MAY   2014

Pebble® Plus

Cheerleading

Cheer Skills

by Jen Jones

Consulting Editor: Gail Saunders-Smith, PhD

Consultant: Lindsay Evered-Ceilley
Director of Business Operations,
Centerstage Starz Theatre and Dance Studio
Centennial, Colorado

CAPSTONE PRESS
a capstone imprint

Pebble Plus is published by Capstone Press,
1710 Roe Crest Drive, North Mankato, Minnesota 56003.
www.capstonepub.com

Books published by Capstone Press are manufactured with paper
containing at least 10 percent post-consumer waste.

Library of Congress Cataloging-in-Publication Data
Jones, Jen.
Cheer skills / by Jen Jones.
p. cm.—(Pebble plus. Cheerleading)
Includes bibliographical references and index.
ISBN 978-1-4296-5276-6 (library binding)
1. Cheerleading—Juvenile literature. I. Title. II. Series.
LB3635.J6325 2011
791.6'4—dc22   2010028061

Editorial Credits
Jenny Marks, editor; Ashlee Suker, designer; Wanda Winch, media researcher; Laura Manthe, production specialist;
    Sarah Schuette, photo stylist; Marcy Morin, scheduler

Photo Credits
All photos Capstone Studio/Karon Dubke except: Shutterstock/Ekaterina Shavaygert, glitter background, Shutterstock/
    Molodec, star background

Note to Parents and Teachers

The Cheerleading series supports national physical education standards related to movement
forms. This book describes and illustrates cheerleading skills. The images support early readers
in understanding the text. The repetition of words and phrases helps early readers learn new
words. This book also introduces early readers to subject-specific vocabulary words, which are
defined in the Glossary section. Early readers may need assistance to read some words and to
use the Table of Contents, Glossary, Read More, Internet Sites, and Index sections of the book.

Printed in the United States of America in North Mankato, Minnesota.
012012
006536CGVMI

Table of Contents

Dazzling Skills

Cheerleaders dazzle
the crowd with cool moves
and school spirit. How do
they do it? They've got skills!

Speak Up

Cheerleaders are loud,

but they don't scream.

Strong, clear, low voices

sound louder than

high voices.

Move It

Cheerleaders' moves are called motions. Some motions look like letters, like K and T. Punches have one hand raised and one on the hips.

There are two V motions.
Low V arms point to the floor
in a V shape. In a high V,
arms are held overhead.

Jump and Tumble

A tuck jump is easy to learn.

Jump straight up. Pull your

knees up to your chest.

Land with your feet together.

A toe touch is another jump.
Lift your legs up and out to
the sides. Reach toward your
toes, but keep your head up.
Your back stays straight.

Cheerleaders also tumble.

A roundoff is like a cartwheel.

While your legs are in the air,

pull your feet together.

Land on both feet at once.

In the Spotlight

Cheerleaders perform fun,

upbeat dance moves.

In a ripple, each cheerleader

does the same motion, one

after the other.

19

Can you guess a cheerleader's

most important skill?

It's not a cartwheel, high kick,

or loud voice. It's a smile!

C-H-E-E-R!

Glossary

dazzle—to amaze

motion—a cheerleading movement

perform—to cheer, sing, stunt, or dance in front of others

spirit—a feeling of excitement and pride

tumble—to do gymnastics moves

upbeat—having a good beat and a fun, catchy tune

Read More

Jones, Christianne C. *Rah-Rah Ruby!* My First Graphic Novel. Mankato, Minn.: Stone Arch Books, 2009.

Karapetkova, Holly. *Cheerleading.* Sports for Sprouts. Vero Beach, Fla.: Rourke Pub., 2010.

Salas, Laura Purdie. *P Is for Pom Pom! A Cheerleading Alphabet.* Alphabet Fun. Mankato, Minn.: Capstone Press, 2010.

Internet Sites

FactHound offers a safe, fun way to find Internet sites related to this book. All of the sites on FactHound have been researched by our staff.

Here's all you do:

Visit *www.facthound.com*

Type in this code: 9781429652766

Super-cool stuff! Check out projects, games and lots more at **www.capstonekids.com**

Index

Word Count: 198
Grade: 1
Early-Intervention Level: 14